Spectacular Sports

Playing Like a Girl

Problem Solving

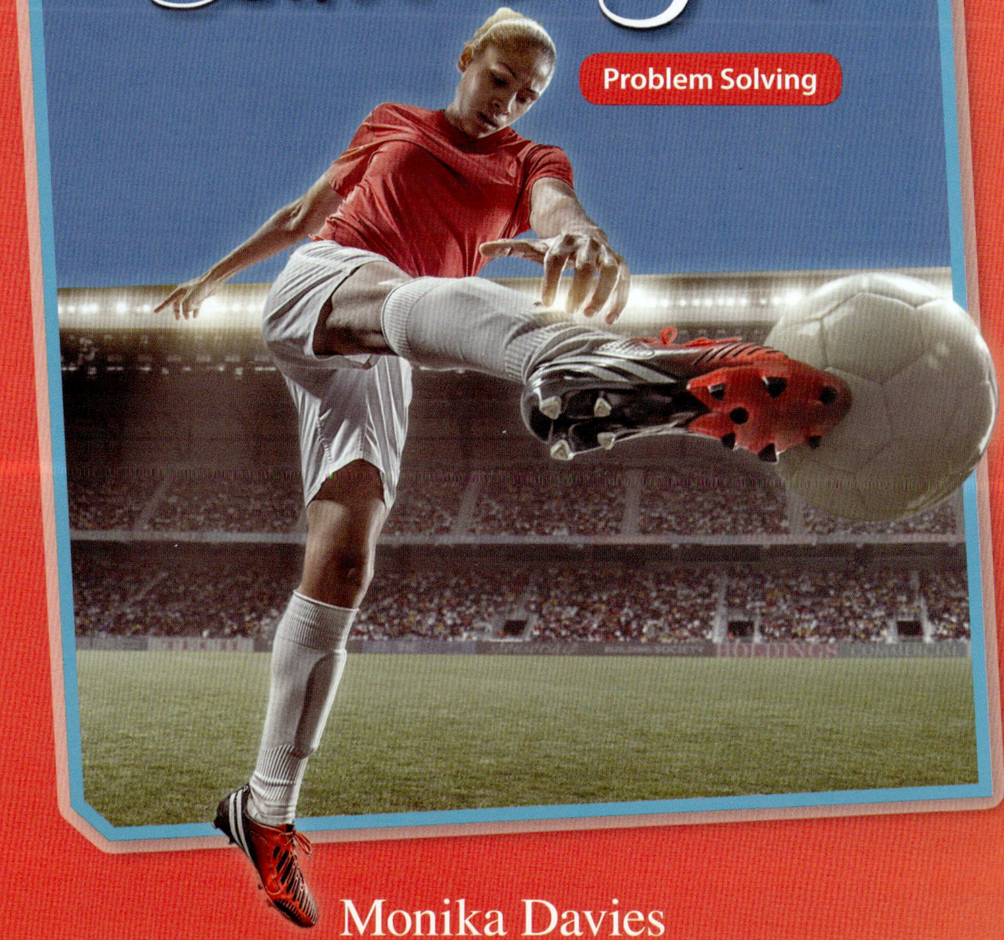

Monika Davies

Consultants

Michele Ogden, Ed.D
Principal
Irvine Unified School District

Colleen Pollitt, M.A.Ed.
Math Support Teacher
Howard County Public Schools

Publishing Credits

Rachelle Cracchiolo, M.S.Ed., *Publisher*
Conni Medina, M.A.Ed., *Managing Editor*
Dona Herweck Rice, *Series Developer*
Emily R. Smith, M.A.Ed., *Series Developer*
Diana Kenney, M.A.Ed., NBCT, *Content Director*
Stacy Monsman, M.A., *Editor*
Kevin Panter, *Graphic Designer*

Image Credits: p.4 Keystone Pictures USA/Alamy Stock Photo; p.6 Jonathan Larsen/Diadem Images/Alamy Stock Photo; p.7 PCN Photography/Alamy Stock Photo; p.8 Xinhua/Alamy Stock Photo; pp.8–9 Matt Jacques/Alamy Stock Photo; pp.10, 11 PCN Photography/Alamy Stock Photo; p.12 Reuters/Alamy Stock Photo; p.13 Joe Rimkus Jr./KRT/Newscom; pp.14–15 Gary Hershorn/Reuters; pp.16–17 David Madison/Getty Images; p.17 Interfoto/Alamy Stock Photo; p.19 Adrees Latif/Reuters/Newscom; p.21 Focus on Sport/Getty Images; p.22 PA Images/Alamy Stock Photo; p.23 Ken Levine/Allsport/Getty Images; all other images from iStock and/or Shutterstock.

Library of Congress Cataloging-in-Publication Data

Names: Davies, Monika, author.
Title: Spectacular sports : playing like a girl / Monika Davies.
Description: Huntington Beach, CA : Teacher Created Materials, [2018] | Includes index. | Audience: Grade 4 to 6.
Identifiers: LCCN 2017011889 (print) | LCCN 2017029812 (ebook) | ISBN 9781480759343 (eBook) | ISBN 9781425855529 (pbk.)
Subjects: LCSH: Sports for girls--Juvenile literature. | Women athletes--Juvenile literature. | Problem solving--Study and teaching (Elementary)--Juvenile literature.
Classification: LCC GV709 (ebook) | LCC GV709 .D37 2018 (print) | DDC 796.082--dc23
LC record available at https://lccn.loc.gov/2017011889

Teacher Created Materials
5301 Oceanus Drive
Huntington Beach, CA 92649-1030
http://www.tcmpub.com

ISBN 978-1-4258-5552-9

Printed by 51250
PO48266 / Printed in USA

Table of Contents

Play Like a Girl

> "This is the century of women."
> —Billie Jean King

When you hear the phrase "you play like a girl," what do you think it means? Do you think it is a compliment? Some of the greatest athletes in the world are women. Yet, it can be a challenge to find news articles about female athletes. There are many more reports about men's sports.

Female athletes are some of the toughest people out there. Every day, no matter the sport, they train. They learn. They work. They strive to be better than they were yesterday.

Explore any sport, and you will find female players that have taken that sport to new heights. Some still compete today, while others played decades ago. These athletes have taken the old insult of "playing like a girl" and have turned it on its head. They have grit—passion and perseverance that help them achieve their goals.

From soccer to tennis to basketball, there are amazing female athletes competing every day.

Billie Jean King competes in 1975 at Wimbledon, the oldest tennis tournament in the world.

Sprinters leave their starting blocks.

LET'S EXPLORE MATH

Before a game, every athlete creates a game plan. The same should be true for every mathlete trying to solve a word problem (that's you!). Match each description to the correct step of this problem-solving plan.

1. Think	**A.** Read and reread the problem.
2. Plan	**B.** Determine whether your solution makes sense.
3. Solve	**C.** Show the solution to the problem.
4. Check	**D.** Decide which strategy to use.

Rising Soccer Star

> "When someone tells me I can't do something, I'm going to always prove them wrong. That's what champions do."
>
> —Carli Lloyd

It's 2015. Over 750 million people are watching the biggest soccer game of the year. They are hoping for a win. They are also hoping for a star player to rise up. Enter Carli Lloyd.

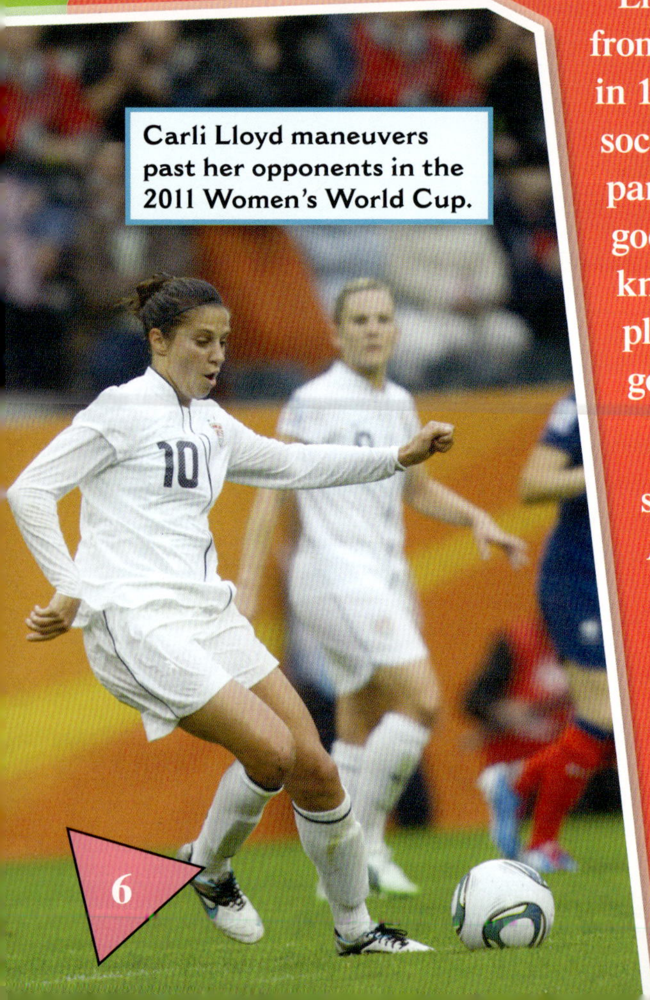

Carli Lloyd maneuvers past her opponents in the 2011 Women's World Cup.

Lloyd, a five-foot-seven midfielder from Delran, New Jersey, was born in 1982. Lloyd kicked her first soccer ball at the age of five. Her parents thought she might be a good ballet dancer. But, Lloyd knew she was meant to be a soccer player. She has been kicking goals ever since.

Yet, Lloyd's road to soccer stardom has had speed bumps. As a young player, she was cut from the U.S. Women's National Team. Lloyd was disappointed. She thought about quitting.

Lloyd maintains possession of the ball at the 2012 Olympic Games.

LET'S EXPLORE MATH

Itzel and her sister have won numerous medals for playing soccer. Itzel has 18 medals. Her sister has 12 medals. If they hang the medals in 2 equal rows, how many will be in each row? Plan how you will tackle this problem. Then, estimate to check that your solution is reasonable.

Think	**Plan**
Solve	**Check**

Then, Lloyd met her trainer, James Galanis. He knew she had talent. But, she needed to be fully committed to improving her skills. The pair began working together. Slowly, Lloyd got stronger—and faster. She soon regained her position on the U.S. team. Her debut on the world stage was in 2005. Since then, she has played for the U.S. soccer team as a center midfielder.

The 2015 World Cup final was a pivotal moment for Lloyd. It was turning into a game for the history books. In the first 16 minutes, Lloyd scored 3 goals. This was the first World Cup **hat trick** scored by a woman! It was a strong start for the U.S. team. Japan's team never recovered.

Lloyd's team ended the game with a 5–2 victory. Her hat trick was a vital part of the win. She won the Golden Ball Award for her performance.

Lloyd is on her way to being one of the world's best soccer players. Remember her name—you will surely hear it again!

Lloyd is awarded the Golden Ball at the 2015 Women's World Cup.

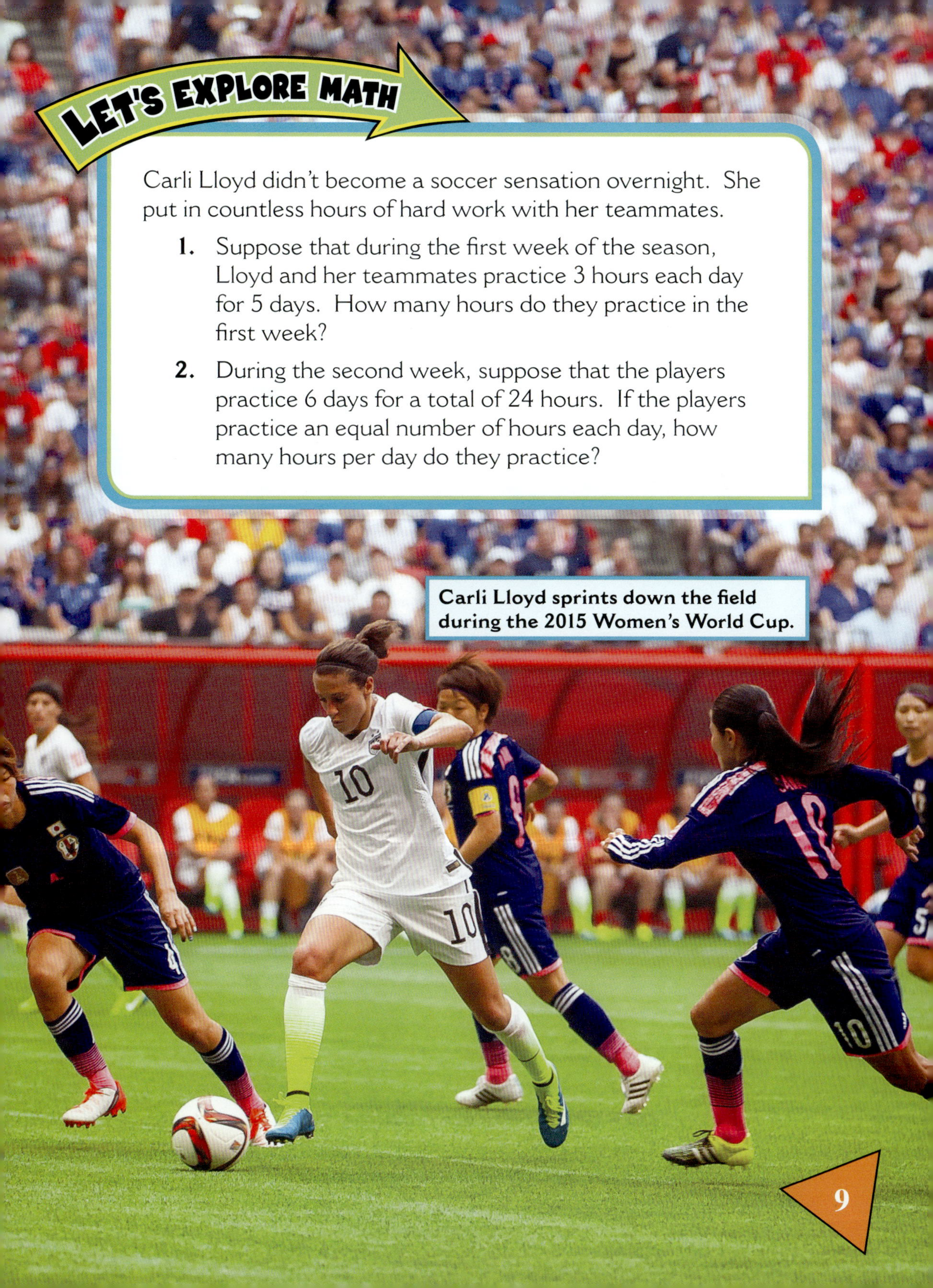

LET'S EXPLORE MATH

Carli Lloyd didn't become a soccer sensation overnight. She put in countless hours of hard work with her teammates.

1. Suppose that during the first week of the season, Lloyd and her teammates practice 3 hours each day for 5 days. How many hours do they practice in the first week?
2. During the second week, suppose that the players practice 6 days for a total of 24 hours. If the players practice an equal number of hours each day, how many hours per day do they practice?

Carli Lloyd sprints down the field during the 2015 Women's World Cup.

Michelle Kwan glides across the ice at the 1998 Winter Olympic Games.

Poetry on Ice

> "Literally falling on the ice and having to pick yourself up in front of thousands of people is not an easy thing to do. The thing that you learn is to pick yourself back up, to learn from your mistakes."
>
> —Michelle Kwan

Graceful, *fierce*, and *strong* are just a few of the words that have been used to describe Michelle Kwan. When she skated, people could barely hear her blades cutting into the ice. She glided with her music. People stood and cheered when she completed her programs.

Before Kwan was a famous skater, she was just a little girl who loved to skate. Kwan's parents immigrated to the United States from Hong Kong. She was born in California in 1980. She is the youngest of three children. Growing up, she watched her brother play ice hockey. Like Lloyd, Kwan was just five years old when she laced up her skates for the first time. After that, she was never too far from an ice rink.

Kwan competes at the 1993 Skate America competition.

It was clear Kwan was going to be a brilliant skater. She won her first competition after two years of practice. At the age of 13, she was the alternate for the U.S. Olympic team. Kwan was young, but she worked hard. Her talent was getting noticed.

In 1998, Kwan headed to the Olympics. She was the favorite to win gold. However, another skater won. Kwan was disappointed. A lot of her fans also shared her sadness. But she said, "I didn't lose the gold. I won the silver."

Kwan's list of victories grew long. She won more than 40 championships. This included five world titles. Although she never won Olympic gold, she had many triumphs. Figure skating careers are often short. But, Kwan skated for many years. During that time, she skated with grace. She faced her losses with a positive attitude. People still talk about her **sportsmanship**. She had the heart and spirit of a true champion.

Michelle Kwan practices a split jump.

Kwan performs her free skate routine at the 2002 Winter Olympic Games.

LET'S EXPLORE MATH

At the beginning of an ice skating competition, there are 40 skaters. Sadly, 3 skaters are injured and must drop out. The remaining skaters are scheduled in groups of 4. Will the groups have an equal number of skaters? Explain your thinking.

A Golden Athlete

> "It is better to look ahead and prepare than to look back and regret."
>
> —Jackie Joyner-Kersee

Sports Illustrated named Jackie Joyner-Kersee the twentieth century's greatest female athlete. It's a bold statement. But many say that it's true.

Joyner-Kersee was born in 1962. It was obvious from the start she could take on any sport. She excelled in track events. She was also skilled at basketball and volleyball. In high school, she completed a 6.68-meter (21.92-foot) jump. It was a state high school record. She was on track to become a star!

But hurdles on the track were not the only challenges Joyner-Kersee would face. While in college, she found out she had severe asthma. At times, she had trouble breathing. Running was a part of her daily life. She worried this would set her back. So, she hid her asthma. Finally, she told her coaches about her condition. She took medication. In the end, her asthma was a hurdle she was able to jump!

Jackie Joyner-Kersee jumps over a hurdle at the 1993 World Championships.

Joyner-Kersee is famous for her **heptathlon** triumphs. A heptathlon has seven events. Points are given for each event. These events last two days. The first day has 100-meter hurdles and the high jump. Next are **shot put** and a 200-meter run. The second day continues with the long jump and **javelin** throw. The day ends with an 800-meter run.

To win, athletes have to be good at all track-and-field events. They must have **stamina**. They do not have to win every event. But, they must do well in each to score points.

Jackie Joyner-Kersee prepares for the javelin throw at the 1996 USA Track and Field Olympic Trials.

Joyner-Kersee competes in the high jump at the 1993 World Championships.

Joyner-Kersee was the first woman to score over 7,000 points in the heptathlon. She scored 7,291 points. She still holds the world record for most points scored. This is why she is known as the best all-around female athlete. She went far in this intense sport. Joyner-Kersee also competed in the Olympics. She won six Olympic medals. Two were for the heptathlon. She truly was unstoppable!

She Shoots, She Scores!

> "Winning is the way you conduct yourself; it's the way you take on every single day in practice...It's a mind-set."
>
> —Diana Taurasi

Diana Taurasi, a six-foot-tall guard, started her basketball career at a young age. In high school, she received the Cheryl Miller Award. This award goes to the best basketball player in Southern California. She continued her career at the University of Connecticut. She led her team to three championships in a row!

Taurasi started playing in the Women's National Basketball Association (WNBA) in 2004. Since then, she has gone on to win many awards. She has won Olympic gold medals, NCAA Championships, and a WNBA Championship. Taurasi is one of nine women to have done this! In 2016, she reached 7,000 career points. She is only the third WNBA player to reach that goal!

Many say Taurasi is different on and off the court. On the court, she's ready to battle. Off the court, she sports a huge grin. Winning and teamwork are more important to her than fame. Fans love her, too! In 2001, she was voted one of the WNBA's Top 15 Players of All Time.

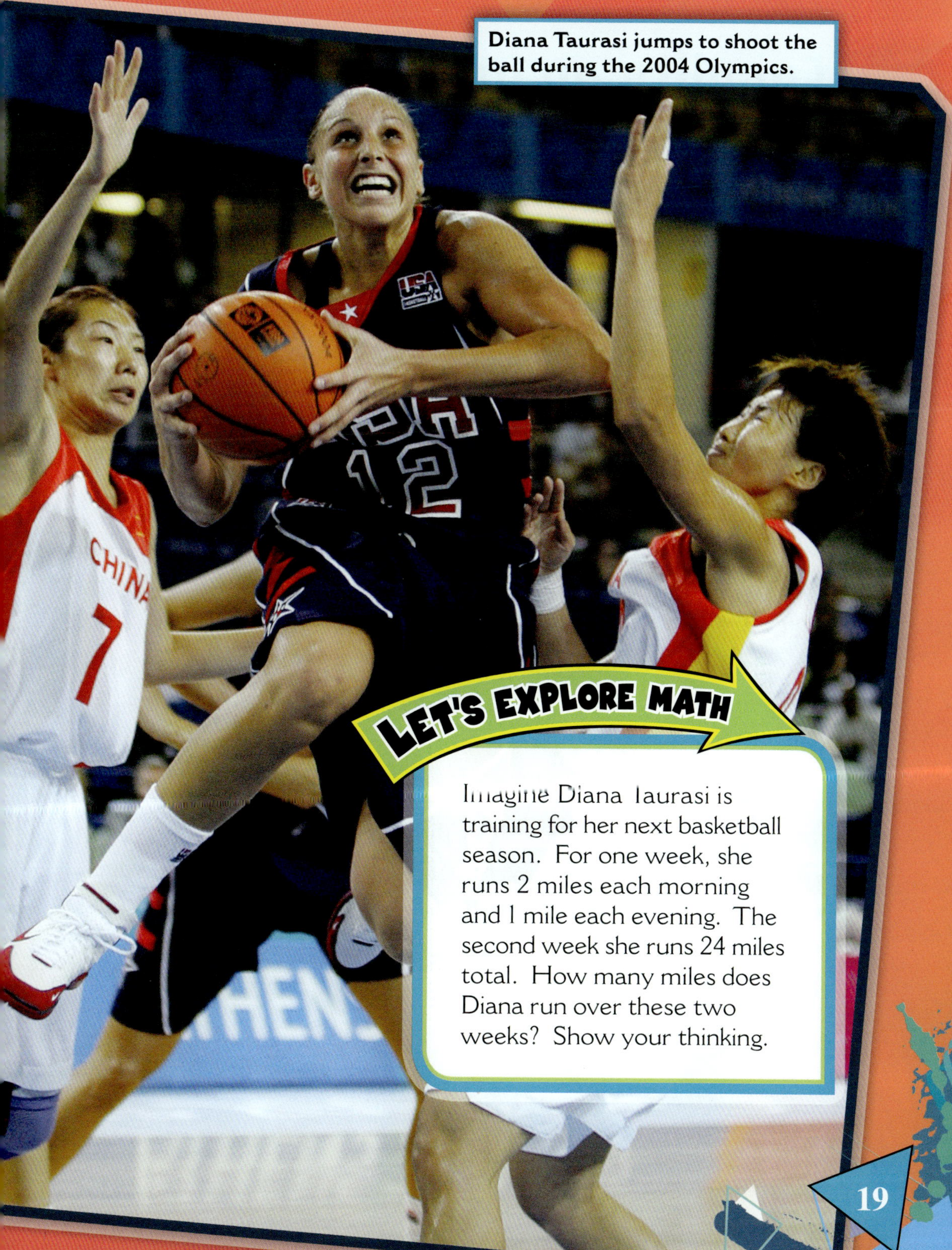

Diana Taurasi jumps to shoot the ball during the 2004 Olympics.

LET'S EXPLORE MATH

Imagine Diana Taurasi is training for her next basketball season. For one week, she runs 2 miles each morning and 1 mile each evening. The second week she runs 24 miles total. How many miles does Diana run over these two weeks? Show your thinking.

Equality on and off the Court

> "The main thing is to care. Care very hard, even if it is only a game you are playing."
>
> —Billie Jean King

Billie Jean King won 39 Grand Slam titles. Grand Slams are the biggest tennis tournaments in the world. These include the Australian Open, the French Open, Wimbledon, and the U.S. Open. King played hard for each and every win. But, her biggest matches were often off the court.

King played in an earlier era. Female players were even less valued and underpaid than they are now. King wanted to change that. In 1973, she helped organize the first women's tennis tour. She also wanted the U.S. Open to award men and women equal prize money. King told officials she would boycott matches if this did not happen. It was a tense time. In the end, she won the **standoff**. It was a victory for women everywhere.

King is also remembered for the "Battle of the Sexes." In 1973, a male tennis player challenged female tennis players to matches. He beat his first female opponent. Then, he came up against King. He thought he could defeat and embarrass her. Instead, she beat him.

LET'S EXPLORE MATH

Billie Jean King played on a standard-sized tennis court that measured 78 feet by 27 feet. How much area did the court cover? Multiply the length by the width using this equation:

$$78 \times 27 = \_\_\_\_\_\_\_\_$$

Billie Jean King returns a shot during the 1970 Wimbledon Championships.

Game, Set, Match

> "As a black tennis player, I looked different. I sounded different. I dressed differently. I served differently. But when I stepped onto the court, I could compete with anyone."
>
> —Serena Williams

Before Billie Jean King retired in 1990, another tennis star was born. Serena Williams served her first tennis ball at the age of four. Her father taught her and her older sister, Venus, how to play tennis. He knew they had the skills to go far. He practiced with them for two hours every day.

But, their father knew they needed better coaching. So, he moved the family to West Palm Beach, Florida. It was there the sisters attended tennis school. It was a smart move. Soon, Williams was winning match after match.

Serena Williams competes in the 2000 Australian Open.

Venus and Serena Williams pose for a photo with President Ronald Reagan in 1990.

Williams turned **pro** in 1995. She quickly began to climb the ranks. Both Williams and her sister were powerful on the court. They played fiercely. Both dominated. No one had seen players like them before!

Serena Williams sinks to one knee to make a shot during the 2015 U.S. Open.

Williams is still one of the most dominant tennis players in the world. She has won all four major Grand Slam titles in a row. This **feat** has been named the "Serena Slam."

Now in her 30s, Williams shows no signs of slowing down. While most tennis players **peak** in their 20s, Williams has become stronger. For Williams, being number one is a goal she has reached. But she is still driven to do her best.

Serena Williams is one of the greats in the tennis world. She has many trophies to prove it. But, her success is more than wins on the court. She also formed the Serena Williams Foundation. She gives scholarships to students in need across the United States.

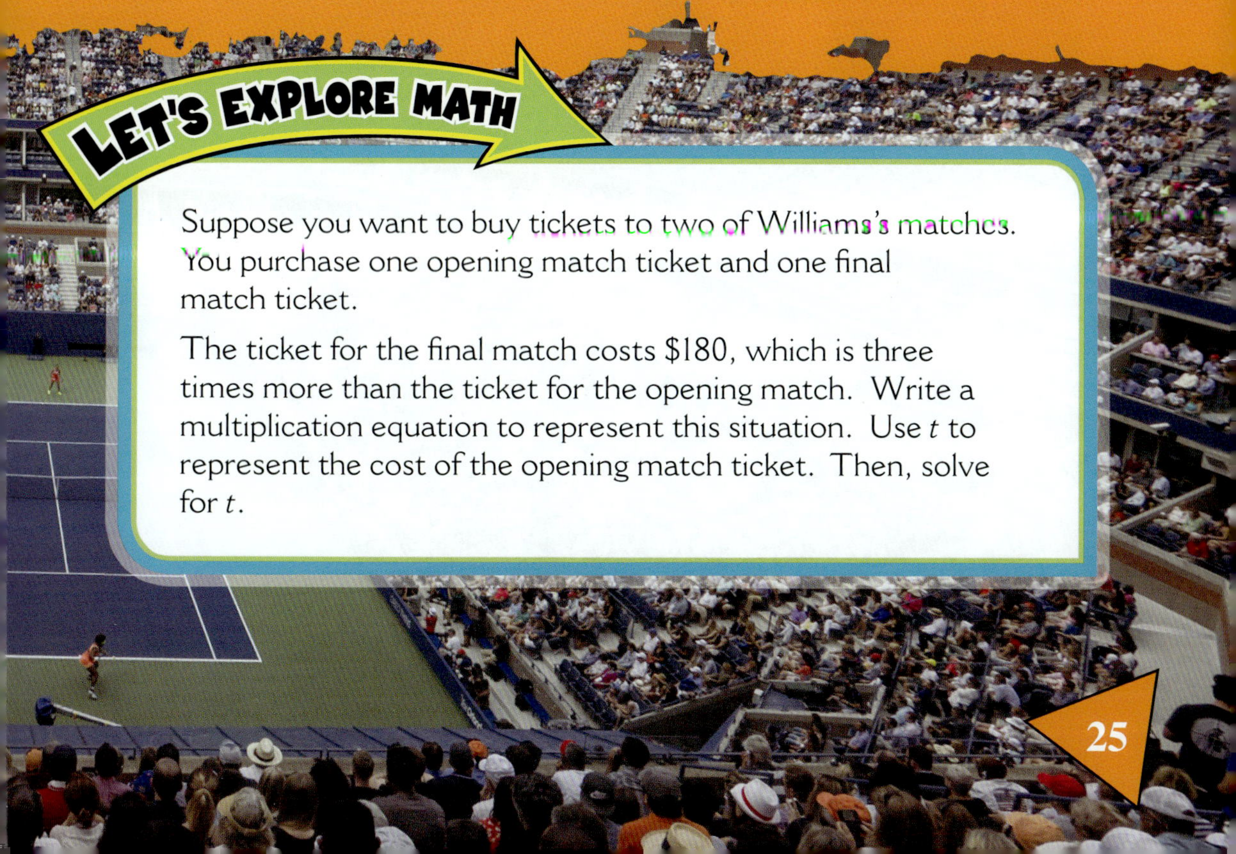

LET'S EXPLORE MATH

Suppose you want to buy tickets to two of Williams's matches. You purchase one opening match ticket and one final match ticket.

The ticket for the final match costs $180, which is three times more than the ticket for the opening match. Write a multiplication equation to represent this situation. Use t to represent the cost of the opening match ticket. Then, solve for t.

Gold medalist Simone Biles lands a vault at the 2016 Olympic Games.

Sport Icons

> "The success of every woman should be the inspiration to another. We should raise each other up. Make sure you're very courageous: be strong, be extremely kind, and above all, be humble."
>
> —Serena Williams

Telling someone "you play like a girl" is the ultimate compliment! It means you are not afraid to make a mistake. You always do your best. You are confident. You are healthy. You are strong. Anyone should be proud to play like a girl!

Every athlete has a similar path to success. Athletes start with a dream, and then they put in the hours of work needed to reach the top!

Female icons of the sporting world are willing to run, skate, and sprint the extra mile. These are the athletes who will be celebrated in our history books. They are the ones who remind us that, with a little grit, we can accomplish any goal.

Problem Solving

Imagine that Serena Williams, Michelle Kwan, Carli Lloyd, Jackie Joyner-Kersee, Diana Taurasi, and Billie Jean King have been invited to compete in a miniature golf tournament. The winner will donate the $50,000 prize money to a charity.

There are 18 holes on the course. Players are allowed only 5 strokes per hole; otherwise, they will be disqualified.

Use the clues on the next page to find each player's score. Then, rank the players from first place to sixth place. Remember, the fewer strokes, the better!

- Kwan makes 6 holes-in-one. After that, it takes her 3 strokes per hole to finish the course.

- King finishes with a score that is equal to the stroke limit.

- King takes three times as many strokes as Joyner-Kersee.

- Lloyd finishes the course with twice as many strokes as Joyner-Kersee.

- Taurasi sinks a hole-in-one and takes 2 strokes for each of the next 2 holes. She takes 6 strokes on the fourth hole and gets disqualified.

- Williams takes 2 strokes per hole for the first 6 holes and 3 strokes for each of the remaining holes.

Glossary

bold—very confident

feat—achievement

hat trick—the scoring of three goals in a game

heptathlon—athletic contest that includes seven events, such as running, jumping, and throwing

javelin—a long spear

peak—the highest level or degree

pro—paid to play a sport

shot put—an event where athletes throw a heavy metal ball as far as they can

sportsmanship—fair and respectful behavior by a competitor

stamina—considerable physical (or mental) strength that holds up for a long period of time

standoff—an argument in which neither side has won yet

Index

Answer Key

Let's Explore Math

page 5:

1. A
2. D
3. C
4. B

page 7:

Estimate: 15 medals; $20 + 10 = 30$; $30 \div 2 = 15$; actual: 15 medals; $18 + 12 = 30$; $30 \div 2 = 15$ or $(18 \div 2) + (12 \div 2) = 15$

page 9:

1. 15 hours; $3 \times 5 = 15$
2. 4 hours; $24 \div 6 = 4$

page 13:

No; $40 - 3 = 37$; $37 \div 4 = 9$ r. 1; Explanations will vary, but should include that skaters can make 9 equal groups of 4 with 1 skater left over.

page 19:

45 miles; $3 \times 7 = 21$; $21 + 24 = 45$

page 21:

2,106 square feet. Strategies will vary.

page 25:

$3 \times t = 180$; $t = \$60$; $180 \div 3 = 60$

Problem Solving

1st: Joyner-Kersee, 30 strokes

2nd: Kwan, 42 strokes

3rd: Williams, 48 strokes

4th: Lloyd, 60 strokes

5th: King, 90 strokes

6th: Taurasi, 11 strokes, but disqualified